Retail Arbitrage For Beginners:

Buy Items at Local Stores and Resell Them Online For Nice Profits

By

Dale Blake

Table of Contents

Introduction 5

Chapter 1. What is Retail Arbitrage? 6

Chapter 2. Where to Buy 8

Chapter 3. What to Buy 13

Chapter 4. A Numbers Game 17

Chapter 5. Time and Space 20

Chapter 6. Where to Sell 24

Chapter 7. About Apps 27

Final Words 28

Thank You Page 30

Retail Arbitrage For Beginners: Buy Items at Local Stores and Resell Them Online For Nice Profits

By Dale Blake

© Copyright 2015 Dale Blake

Reproduction or translation of any part of this work beyond that permitted by section 107 or 108 of the 1976 United States Copyright Act without permission of the copyright owner is unlawful. Requests for permission or further information should be addressed to the author.

This publication is designed to provide accurate and authoritative information in regard to the subject matter covered. This work is sold with the understanding that the publisher is not engaged in rendering legal, accounting, or other professional services. If legal advice or other expert assistance is required, the services of a competent professional person should be sought.

First Published, 2015

Printed in the United States of America

Introduction

Every day, people make tens and hundreds of dollars as amateur retail arbitrage sellers. The changing face of the global economy, effected by the internet and increased ability to ship quickly and reliably worldwide, has empowered people to take charge of their own earnings with simple retail arbitrage. You too can take advantage of these factors and put yourself in the driver's seat of your own finances. It doesn't require any special tools or skills, and with just a little bit of knowledge, you can begin your journey. Fortunately, even if there's a lot to learn in the long run, you'll be making money as you go. So, with nothing to lose, and plenty to gain (nothing less than economic independence) you may as well get started.

Chapter 1. What is Retail Arbitrage?

Arbitrage itself is nothing new. That old axiom "buy low sell high" is the essential basis of the concept of arbitrage. Arbitrage is a concept wherein the main party serves as an intermediary in a 'no risk' transaction. While true arbitrage is risk free, that is simply a theoretical concept. In reality there is the risk of devaluation, but this can be mitigated. In successful arbitrage, the value of the product is known and is stable. The buyer then ensures that the resale will bring a profit. The trick to arbitrage is to be certain that the effort of the transaction is valued at the rate of return.

Retail arbitrage applies this concept to a retail setting. Retail arbitrage is the act of purchasing an actual product at a retail location, and then reselling that same product at a profit. This, as well, is nothing new. What is new, is the universe of opportunity available to anyone with an internet connection. The scope of retail arbitrage possibilities now extends to a global market which means that with some creative thinking, you have a nearly limitless client base. This means you can extend well beyond your own area, and thereby turn your local conditions (which can be inhibitive of successful arbitrage) into a boon for your business.

The basic concept of retail arbitrage is that you buy something near you, and sell it somewhere else at a profit. Now, you may be able to buy and sell in the same area, but extending beyond your own area makes it much easier to create the price differential necessary for profit. The places you buy, the items you choose, the markets you sell to, all matter as far as your success goes. There are many other factors as well, but let's get into this one step at a time. In the end, you have a basic working knowledge of how to make money working for yourself in the field of retail arbitrage.

Chapter 2. Where to Buy

You need to be paying something below average retail if you hope to make profits in retail arbitrage. The notion of where you are extends from your corner shop, all the way to what country you live in. You'll find a zone of influence appropriate for your skills and how hard you want to work, and you'll make money doing it. So let's consider the stores in your neighborhood as a good starting point.

Thrift, Goodwill, etc.

These stores are the bargain hunter's jungle. They are full of useless junk, and worthless items. At the same time, there's a wealth of treasures in these stores. First off, we need to separate two major concepts, and that is big ticket versus small ticket items. You may find some precious antique in a thrift shop and sell it for many times what you paid for it. That's a great thing to hope for, but it's not typical reality. In the Retail arbitrage game (it helps to think of it as a game) these finds that sell for 700% or more of purchase price are called a home-run and it doesn't happen every day. What you want to look for in the thrift shops are those small inexpensive items which will sell for double what you pay for it. That means buying a T-shirt for five dollars and selling it for ten. That's profit and you'll need to start thinking in those terms in order to develop the right mindset for a successful gambit at arbitrage.

Books are a tricky one, and most people don't arbitrage them. For one, prices aren't great, the market is limited, and they are heavy (expensive) to ship. One exception might be sets of children's books, or any other complete set. Again, shipping costs are high, but if you can manage to find it cheap enough and in decent quality, you might still turn a profit.

With a bit of research, you'll start to understand which items consistently sell. You'll develop an eye for the things you want, and you'll also develop your own style. Will you be a generalist? Will you specialize in some particular genre? Either way, your trips to thrift and goodwill will change as your acumen develops. Soon you'll be scanning these stores in minutes and scheduling trips to visit every store in your area.

Big Boxes and Cheap Prices

Chances are good that regardless of where you live, there's one of the large discount stores near you. These stores are already priced pretty low, and they regularly put items in clearance which can put you in the money even faster. Wal-Mart, Costco, Target, Big Lots, Hobby Lobby, Sears, Kmart, Office Supply, or any other store that specializes in cheap goods, will be a solid source of items for your arbitrage.

Now something important to consider is the level of profit you might make. When purchasing mass produced items, you need to be looking for a significant price difference (300% or more) in order to make it worthwhile. That's because there are so many available and competition is so high, that you have to have a good price to make a quick sale. On the plus side though, there are literally thousands of items you can arbitrage from these big discount stores.

When at these stores, you'll typically go right past normal items, and you'll quickly learn to blow right past 'sale' items as well. The reason is that unless you are talking about a unique item (more on this later) there just isn't enough of a profit margin for you. By the time you purchase, list, sell, and ship those items, you may have cut into your profits to the point that you're wasting your time. So what you'll want to do is to head for clearance.

Clearance is one of the easiest and best ways to start making money right away. But don't think that just because it says 'clearance' that you are actually getting a good deal. One pro-tip for you is that a phone application makes all the difference in the world. Phone apps allow you to scan a USB barcode while you're in the store, and they will tell you the average price of that item as it sells on eBay or Amazon (there are many apps available, choose one that matches your style). By using one of these applications you can instantly identify those items that offer you a 300% return on your merchandise. Clearance in one store is different than the next, so plan a long day of strolling the aisles while scanning code after code. In time, you'll develop a good sense for a variety of items.

Mom and Pop Shops

While not typically the best for value, you still may decide to include these stores in your arbitrage adventures. The reason they can be valuable to you is that they often carry unique items that can turn a real profit if you market them in the right place at the right time. Art, tools, decorative items, books, and other more specialty items can all be found at value in these stores. The tricky part here is that you'll need some personal knowledge of the value fluctuations of these items across the spectrum of your sales market.

Yard Sales, etc.

Much like thrift shops, yard sales, garage sales, flea markets, etc may offer you the chance to find items that are amazingly mispriced. You can find real steals when the seller doesn't know what a gem they've got. Again, you'll need some sense of what you're looking at, but there are some great items you can expect to find. Video games, puzzles, toys, decorations, and anything vintage will all be big sellers. What is old junk at a garage sale can easily become a huge find to your buyer over eBay or Amazon. Probably, in the long run, you'll make the most money through your yard/garage sales days. With a bit of practice, you can easily be pulling $100 days by hitting just a few garage sales. One tip though, the early bird gets the worm!

Chapter 3. What to Buy

Your choice of which items you will arbitrage will depend on your preferences, your knowledge, what's available to you in your area, and how hard you want to work. Again, a good phone application will give you the real-time knowledge that you'll need to make informed decisions on the fly. Always remember the 3X rule (that the item *must* sell for more than 3 times what you pay) Many new arbitrageurs start off thinking they can make up in volume what they lose on value, but that's an expensive lesson to learn. What the new arbitrager quickly learns is that buying is the fun part, counting money is even better, but that posting your items for sale can become tedious and tiring. To stay motivated, and make the most of your time, you need a good return on your items. Selling at 3 times the purchase price should be your guideline as a bare minimum if you are planning to bulk arbitrage. Now, that rule changes if you are looking at a single big-ticket item, but that's more of a specialty. If you just want to generate a livable income by shopping and selling, then you should focus on small, inexpensive items that you can buy and flip fast.

Children's toys, new in box, can be a good bet, especially if you play the seasonality game. Purchase simple toys that appeal to everyone. Handheld games, puzzles, baby toys, stuffed animals, and inexpensive sports equipment (really just sports toys) are all pretty good sellers.

Decorations and party favors are another often overlooked. Think about a "Happy Birthday" banner in the discount bin at a discount store. Maybe they have 10 of them and they're fifty cents each. You can easily sell them at three or four dollars. That means you spend $5 to earn $25 profit minimum. The same can be done for bags of balloons, napkins, paper plates, tablecloths etc. with a theme: baby shower, kid's themes, birthday, holidays and occasions, can all be super high value added items. The good thing about party decorations is that they sell all year round, with certain hot times now and again.

Cosmetics and toiletries are great although Amazon.com has a number of policies regarding what can and cannot be sold on their sight. Toiletries like combs, brushes, nail clippers and other nail-care tools, picks, rollers, makeup brushes, etc all sell well. These gains are items that you can sometimes find insanely cheap and turn around for 6-7-or 10 times what you bought them for. This is the type of bulk arbitrage that can really pay off.

Another sure thing is sports paraphernalia. Anything from pencils, to mugs, to clothing and novelties are all hot tickets. Buy them up whenever you find them cheap and you won't be sorry.

If you want to go for big ticket items, or just get lucky with the occasional home-run, then keep an eye out for these treasures. Metal lunchboxes in almost any condition. Old toys and handheld electronic games are always top sellers. Commemorative items typically have a good market. When it comes to art, antiques, jewelry, and other specialty goods, you can always feel free to take a risk, but most arbitrageurs just aren't trying to deal with that kind of hassle.

In the beginning, just rely on your application to get a sense of prices and you'll quickly learn the market. Mid level items like electrical appliances can be tricky, but occasionally you'll find them in working order (with box a bonus) and you might be able to spin them to make it worth it.

Don't let yourself be fooled by the fact that your items are inexpensive…that's where a majority of the money is, and that's what arbitrage is all about.

Chapter 4. A Numbers Game

There are some tricks for thinking when you enter the game, and the first is the concept of cumulative value. In this, you need to count the raindrops (so to speak). If you are moving inventory (and you're careful about what you purchase and list)then that's all profit. Each item you move puts a plus into your account and that's the goal. If you want to make money, you'll need to constantly be buying, listing, selling, and shipping. This is the best way to keep the income stream flowing and enables you to reinvest quickly and grow your trade.

The next concept relates to posting your items. Many newcomers to the game try to think in the number of items they have listed. "Ok, I'll list 50 items a week to start", but that really makes no sense. The way to account for your sales is to think of the amount of profit you have posted. For example, Post $400 worth of merchandise (that's profit not price) and you'll start to see a correlation between posts, sales, and numbers.

Another concept is that you want to be making profit. Most arbitrageurs hold themselves to a minimum $10 profit per sale. This is to mitigate the costs of shipping and fees charged by the sight you sell through. This may seem like a lot at first, but you'll quickly realize that there is a reason that successful arbitrageurs don't go too low.

You need to list items. Lots of items. So, if you follow the above concepts of 3-times your profit, and a $10 minimum, then you will make money. How much money will you make? There is a rough calculations that most successful arbitrageurs hold to and it works simply on numbers.

If you post $100 (profit) each day of the month, then you should expect to make $1,000 that month. It seems arbitrary, but the numbers hold up consistently and if you follow through . Now to be clear, that's listing new items each day. If you're just doing this for some extra money, then it's up to you. But if you want to earn a living (and plenty of people make a living this way) then you have to get serious and list new items every day.

Always think in terms of profit as well as turnaround. If you are buying items and listing each day, but it takes a month to turnover your inventory because you only sell ballet outfits, then you are not realizing your potential. Think in terms of percent profit to you and you'll see more clearly where the bottlenecks are for your arbitrage business.

Chapter 5. Time and Space

In order for arbitrage to work, there must be a price discrepancy that you take advantage of. There are many ways to realize a price discrepancy and to take advantage of that for your own benefit. It takes a new type of thinking to become a successful arbitrager.

We've already discussed the places near you where you can find bargains that meet your criteria, and which types of items you may consider selling. Let's think bigger to help us understand where opportunity lies for you.

Time

Successful arbitrageurs think in quarterly terms just like banks and brokerages. There is a sales cycle and it can be your best friend. Think about post Christmas clearance sales. Lights, decorations, wrapping paper, costumes, themed items like mugs and plates and other decoratives, these all become dirt cheap. One strategy is to buy these up and wait until the third quarter when those items get hot again (also you can list them year round, because some people are always on the lookout for a deal) This strategy goes for any holiday or seasonal event.

Seasons are another great way to take advantage of sales cycles. Buy swimsuits in the winter and sell them in the spring. Buy last year's ski equipment in March and wait until September for the early bargain hunters that are looking to snatch up a deal. Look for seasonal clearance as long as you have the storage capacity to hold over inventory for next year. This is a slow growth strategy, but once you make it through one full cycle, you'll be in the black and back on top.

Hot items are another way to take advantage of time. If you have a chance to buy the new hot thing, then snap it up and wait for the store shelves to empty out. Once they do you'll see the prices on those items going through the roof. The trick here is to sell that item before the factory catches up with demands and floods the stores with a second release. This can be a gamble because trends come and go, and sometimes what was impossible to find becomes mundane (as the factory floods the market) and then you are left holding an item that used to be worth a bundle.

Space

Take advantage of geographic differences and you might be gaining an edge against other arbitrageurs (you're not in competition really, which is another great benefit). Think of it this way: when a snow blower goes on clearance in West Virginia, they are impossible to find in Maine. Think about where you live and what your seasonality can offer you as an advantage. You'll be shocked to see how well you can do just selling wintry items from the discount store in your hometown to those living in the frozen north. In reverse, it looks like this: Beach season ends earlier in New York than it does in North Carolina. Once those items hit the clearance rack, snatch them up and post them. Even if you're just selling to other arbitrageurs on the other end, that still works for you.

Consider, as well, regional needs. Maybe a storm is coming and gas cans are cheap where you live. Maybe It's tools or other construction materials that are cheap in your area because people live in masonry homes and not wood. Think regionally and you might find a market that others are overlooking.

Understand that people living in remote locations make most of their purchases online. Things like tools, clothing, specialty items, and decorative items inflate dramatically in price when they arrive at stores in those areas. Some people make a whole living selling cheap tools and work wear by travelling to all their local depot stores and buying up anything that falls way below expected retail price. If you are careful about what you offer, shipping weights don't even become an issue.

Chapter 6. Where to Sell

Now, there is the potential to sell your wares on a site like Craigslist, but why? That is a regionalized web site which means you'll be posting your item all over the place. That's inefficient, and not very ineffective. There are far better ways to maximize your effort and maximize returns on time spent. The big two are Amazon and eBay and there are benefits and detriments to each.

Amazon

Amazon is probably the best place for a beginner because it has a tutorial that walks you through the process step by step. Really, you could take some item lying around your house right now and post it to Amazon within the hour. The first time might take you a bit if time, but you'll quickly get the hang of it and you'll be flying through your postings in no time. Amazon is particular about which items you can sell, about the condition of the items, and also about how you post, what you post, and how frequently you post. These are just the conditions you'll have to deal with, but it's well worth it because Amazon is user friendly and really streamlines the entire process from posting, to shipping , to getting paid.

eBay

eBay is less particular about what can be sold through their site. This can be good when you want to sell the items that are restricted on Amazon. eBay, however is less easy to navigate and is not tailored specifically for your purposes. But, it's another GIGANTIC source of buyers. Use both sites to maximize your sales potential and you'll see the results come in even faster.

Both of these sites offer a number of options regarding posting, shipping, payments, and guarantees. A more thorough exploration of these sites will enable you to choose the options sets that best suit your needs and expectations. However you expect to be going about your arbitrage, there will be a combination that is perfect for you.

The best way to get started is to go and list several items. If you have a smartphone, it will simplify the process. This is because you can take a picture with your phone, and then upload your photo directly to the site. Either way, go ahead and follow through and list your item. List several items that day until you are fully comfortable with the process. Then you'll be pleased to see how quickly you get a response. From then on, you'll have a good idea of how it works and you'll have the motivation to really get started. Also, you'll realize that the earning potential is up to you. Hard work and diligent will pay off if you stick with it.

Chapter 7. About Apps

An up to date pricing application from your phone makes all the difference. Not only will it help you learn the ropes and pricing, it will eliminating the need to guess. There is an application called Profit Bandit that has become the standard tool for retail arbitrage. Amazon has just come out with their own application, but either way, if that's an option for you, then you should absolutely go ahead and begin using the best tool available to you.

Final Words

Maybe you are looking for a way to supplement your income. Perhaps you've become a victim of the global economic downturn. Maybe you are retired and want something to do. Retail arbitrage is an opportunity for anyone that wants to take the reins of their income. No licensing, no office, no hours, no boss. It's even a great option for stay-at-home moms and dads. It gets you out of the house, keeps your brain active, and has the potential to earn a significant income. Many arbitrageurs who deal only in mundane simple items target $3,500 per month in profit. That's pretty darn good earning power for someone without a 'job'.

Basically, there are price differentials all over the country, all the time. Amazon and Ebay provide a clearinghouse for people to meet and mutually benefit from those differences. Whether you want to play a seasonal market, or take advantage of your geographic region, there's a place for you. If you want to specialize in baby clothes because you know about them, or deal only in collectible cards because that's what you enjoy, there's a place for you. Maybe you go to the major discount stores a few days a week anyway. You can easily clean out the clearance bins and go to work arbitraging for yourself without even making a special trip. Once the money starts coming in, you're spending profits on your next round of items, and from that point on, your business is solvent. Where you grow it from there is entirely your choice, but you might be surprised how far you can go.

Thank You Page

I want to personally thank you for reading my book. I hope you found information in this book useful and I would be very grateful if you could leave your honest review about this book. I certainly want to thank you in advance for doing this.

If you have the time, you can check my other books too.

www.ingramcontent.com/pod-product-compliance
Lightning Source LLC
LaVergne TN
LVHW021747060526
838200LV00052B/3523